HOW BIG IS BIG?

For my children.
– S.S.
To Mom and Cookie.
– F.4.

Canadian Cataloguing in Publication Data
Strauss, Stephen
  How big is big?

Poems.
ISBN 1-55263-017-X

1. Weights and measures – Juvenile poetry. 2. Weights and measures – Miscellanea – Juvenile literature. I. Fernandes, Eugenie, 1943-   . II. Title.

PS8587.T72334H68 1999   jC811'.54   C98-932743-4
PR8587.T72334H68 1999

THE CANADA COUNCIL | LE CONSEIL DES ARTS
FOR THE ARTS | DU CANADA
SINCE 1957 | DEPUIS 1957

The publisher gratefully acknowledges the assistance of the Canada Council and the Ontario Arts Council for its publishing program.

Canada

We acknowledge the financial support of the Government of Canada through the Book Publishing Industry Development Program (BPIDP) for our publishing activities.

Key Porter kids
is an imprint of
Key Porter Books Limited
70 The Esplanade
Toronto, Ontario
Canada M5E 1R2

www.keyporter.com

Design: Kathryn Moore

Printed and bound in Italy

99 00 01 02 03 6 5 4 3 2 1

HOW BIG IS

STEPHEN STRAUSS · THE FERNANDES 4

KPk
Key Porter Kids

HOW BIG IS BIG?

How big is big?
A super fat pig?
A giant tomato?
A skyscraper potato?
No, bigness is something no one can consume,
Like how many oceans
Fit into the moon.

A dust particle is so small that if you put ten of them on top of one another, they would still be about as thin as a dime.

HOW SMALL IS SMALL?

How small is small?
Something minus-feet tall?
The point of a pencil?
The line on a stencil?
No, smallness is something that's quite hard to see,
Like the fluff in the air
And the dust on your chair.

HOW SLOW IS SLOW?

How slow is slow?
As we all know,
A snail in a hurry
Will never scurry,
But glide at the pace
Of a drop of molasses
That drips off your face.

HOW FAST IS FAST?

How fast is fast?
I'm glad *that* you asked.
To walk on water,
You oughta oughta
Use all o' your might,
And double *the* speed
Of a motorbike.

The fastest snail can slither at 27.5 feet (8.4 meters) an hour.

The fastest motorcycle speed is 318 mph (512 km/hr); the speed required to "walk" on water is 671 mph (1080 km/hr).

HOW HIGH IS HIGH?

How high is high?
Well, how high is the sky?
I'll say it out loud:
It's higher than a cloud,
It's where the air plays peek-a-boo,
Changing nighttime's black
To daytime's blue.

Between 125 to 185 miles
(about 200 and 300 km) up
in the sky, the blue sky
color ends and becomes
black.

HOW DEEP IS DEEP?

How deep is deep?
No, I don't mean deep sleep,
And I don't mean a well,
or a deep prison cell;
But rather imagine the fishies' commotion
If a kid ever walked
On the bottom of the ocean.

People have descended
35,814 feet (10,915 meters) into
the ocean. The deepest spot in
the Pacific Ocean is 36,201 feet
(11,034 meters) deep.

HOW LIGHT IS LIGHT?

How light is light?
Well, there's light as a kite...
And do you know whether
That's ten times a feather?
But, oh—I think there's been some mistake!
For both weigh much more
Than a single snowflake.

A chicken feather weighs roughly .0007 ounces (.02 grams), and a snowflake only .00000035 ounces (.000001 grams).

HOW HEAVY IS HEAVY?

How heavy is heavy?
Asked a boy named Levy,
Who decided to buy a dinosaur,
But couldn't carry it out of the store.
So he left instead with a lovely toy lion,
Whose weight, while great,
He could lift without try'n.

The largest dinosaur weighed between 110,000 and 175,000 pounds (50,000 and 80,000 kilograms) while the largest lion weighed in at only 690 lbs (373 kg).

The Pacific Ocean is 12,300 miles (19,800 kilometers) wide and stretches between Indonesia and the coast of Colombia in South America.

HOW WIDE IS WIDE?

How wide is wide?
Well, *there's* wide as outside,
And *there's* wide as a smile,
And *there's* wide as *the* Nile,
But wider by far—sort of wideness *terrific*—
Is *the width of that* ocean
They call *the* Pacific.

HOW STRETCHY IS STRETCHY?

How *stretchy* is *stretchy*?
It may seem far-fetchy,
But spiders, quite scary,
And sometimes quite hairy,
Make stuff so fantastic,
It's totally, totally,
TOTALLY, elastic.

A spider's silk can stretch up to 10 times its original length without breaking. A web made by an American spider has been known to trap a small mouse.

HOW OLD IS OLD?

How old is old?
I have been told
That turtles live long
And trees linger on,
But if true oldness you want to convey,
Then try wishing an amoeba
A happy birthday.

The rhinoceros beetle, which weighs one-tenth of an ounce (only 2.8 grams), can lift 100 times its own weight and walk for a half hour carrying 30 times its own weight! This is like an average-sized man walking one mile (1.6 kilometers) with a car on his head.

HOW STRONG IS STRONG?

How strong is strong?
Consider King Kong,
The movie gorilla,
Whose death was a thrilla.
But even old Kong was monstrously feeble
When compared
To the mighty rhinoceros beetle.

HOW LONG IS LONG?

How long is long?
You'll be long gone
Once the sun
Ceases to run,
And the only light
Is endless, endless,
Starry night.

HOW BRIEF IS BRIEF?

How brief is brief?
Well, it's my belief
That when you blink,
Or slyly wink,
The time that passes
Is much, much more
Than lightning flashes.

A blink takes about one third of a second, and a wink only about a second. A lightning flash takes about a thousandth of a second.

It is estimated that the sun will burn itself out in 5 billion years. You will likely live about 75 years.

If 3.5 billion Pekingese dogs jumped from a ladder that was 6 feet 7 inches high (2 meters), they would create an earthquake measuring about 4.5 on the Richter Scale. That's enough to make anything close by, including cars and trees, start to shake.

HOW SHAKY IS SHAKY?

How shaky is shaky?
Something kinda earthquaky?
If a mountain of Pekingese,
Those dogs love to tease,
Were to jump from a ladder,
They'd make
The ground clatter.

HOW FULL IS FULL?

How full is full?
Not a belly full of wool,
Not a mountain of hay,
Not Santa's toy sleigh.
No, fullness is more like that quenching of thirsting
Which comes to a camel
Whose drunk till she's bursting!

A camel can drink up to 30 U.S. gallons (114 liters) in ten minutes and 50 U.S. gallons (189 liters) over several hours.

HOW HOT IS HOT?

How hot is hot?
How hot you got?
I wouldn't choose
To take off my shoes
And go for a stroll
On a flaming bed
Of burning hot coal.

HOW COLD IS COLD?

How cold is cold?
You'd be quite bold
To stick out your nose,
Or undress your toes,
In any cruel breeze
Cold enough to make
Thermometers freeze.

A mercury thermometer will freeze at -38°F. (-39°C). Your skin will freeze within a half minute at -58°F (-50°C) with a 12 mph (20 km/hr) wind.

HOW SWEET IS SWEET?

How sweet is sweet?
Now *this* poem's a treat.
Though sugar is dandy,
And *it* rhymes with candy,
Little can give such a sweetening rush,
As *the* leaves of a green
South American bush.

The Paraguayan plant *Stevia rubidiana* has leaves that are more than 300 times sweeter than sugar. One teaspoon of *Stevia* is equal to about 6 cups of sugar!

HOW MANY IS MANY?

How many is many?
Two dimes or *ten* pennies?
All grapes in a bunch?
Forty crackers for lunch?
No, many is something beyond stacks and stacks,
It's how much *the* earth weighs
In piles of Big Macs.

If you were to put the earth on a scale, you would need about 27,800,000,000,000,000,000,000,000 Big Macs on the opposite side to balance it.

A bite is 1.25 times more powerful than a karate chop.

HOW CHEWY IS CHEWY?

How chewy is chewy?
What makes gum so gooey?
Each time you bite,
As hard as you might,
The force is so whopping—
Think karate chop, chop,
And *then* keep on chopping.

HOW HARD IS HARD?

How hard is hard?
Who keeps the scorecard?
It's not baby powder,
Nor soupy clam chowder;
It's not an eggshell, a penny, or brass,
But a diamond so hard,
It slices through glass.

A diamond is the hardest thing in the world. It is much, much harder (10,000 times harder, in fact) than your teeth.

HOW THIN IS THIN?

How *thin* is *thin*?
Well, *there's thin* as a pin.
Then *there's thin* as a sliver
(Ouch! sharp *things* make me quiver).
But *thinness* is something *to* measure *with* care;
It's a slice, of a slice,
Of a slice, of a hair.

A slice, of a slice, of a slice of a hair is about .00026 inches (about 6.4 microns) across.

HOW THICK IS THICK?

How *thick* is *thick*?
That question's a *trick!*
Thickness is *thinness*, just *turned* on *its* head,
And one is *the other*, so don't be misled.
I ask you *to take ten* heads full of hair,
Glue one *to another*—
And see *thickness* right *there.*

If you took hair from ten different heads and glued one on top of the other, you'd end up with a pile about 165 feet (50 meters) thick.

On a sunny day after a snowstorm, it is as bright as if you were in a dark closet surrounded by 16,000 lit candles.

HOW BRIGHT IS BRIGHT?

How bright is bright?
Imagine *the* sight
When *the* snow has snowed,
And *the* sun has glowed,
And a little kid sits
Counting 16,000
Candlesticks.

HOW DARK IS DARK?

How dark is dark?
There's as dark as a park
In *the* middle of *the* night,
With no moon in sight,
And a fog billowing billows.
I guarantee
You won't spy armadillos.

If you looked to the sky at midnight on a moonless, overcast night, in a really dense fog, there probably wouldn't be enough light for your eyes to see anything at all.

HOW LOUD IS LOUD?

How loud is loud?
The screams of a crowd?
The snap of your gum?
The bang of a drum?
No, loud is every hurtful noise
That pains the ears
Of girls and boys.

Sound above 130 decibels is painful. That is 100 times louder than the sound of a horn blast from 20 feet (6 meters) away, and roughly twice as loud as the loudest scream.

HOW QUIET IS QUIET?

How quiet is quiet?
Not a schoolyard riot,
Not a loud snore,
And not a dance floor.
No, quiet is something you almost can't hear,
Like the sound that your hair
Keeps away from your ear.

The amount of sound that your hair growing over your ears would block you from hearing is 300 times softer than a whisper.